ARRAN

FOR

FAMILIES

Redshank.

Arran for Families
© David Hilton 2013

Published by David Hilton
1/6 Joppa Station Place,
Edinburgh,
EH15 2QU

ISBN: 978-0-9576956-0-3

Designed by David Hilton

Printed by Martins the Printers
Prepress by Raspberry Creative Type

A copy of this book is on record at The British Library

Ringed Plover.

ARRAN
FOR
FAMILIES

AN ILLUSTRATED JOURNEY ROUND THE ISLAND

by Joyce and David Hilton

FOR

Ben

Laurie

Lucy

Alanna

Paul

Orla

Lewie

Our Grandchildren and our friends.

May the love of the island stay with you for ever

CONTENTS

INTRODUCTION

You have made a wise choice, coming to Arran for your holidays. There is so much to see on this delightful island lying in the Firth of Clyde that you may find it hard to choose what to visit first and not to miss anything.

Primrose

Sea Pink.

When our little grandsons, Ben and Laurie, were staying with us in Whiting Bay, they said we should write our own book with drawings and notes of the places they liked best. This is the result.

Forget-me-not.

Our book is for children, Mums and Dads, Grans and Grandads, and anybody who loves Arran, or is on their first visit. There are also many sharing our love of the island who, maybe, can no longer pay frequent visits. This book could be a present to remind them of all the happy times they have spent here in this special place.

Thistle.

Lady's Smock, or Cuckoo Flower.

Sheep's bit

Ragged Robin

Bird's Foot Trefoil.

THE SECOND EDITION

Five years have passed since "Arran for Families" was published. It has always been good to hear from people who, perhaps, discovered the "Doctor's Bath" or "Hutton's Unconformity" with the help of this book.

Look out for ---SQUIRRELS!

There will always be changes on the island and some of these will make life better for islanders and visitors alike. We shall also miss some familiar things, especially if we remember them from our childhood holidays. The Postbus no longer carries passengers. You cannot now count the steps to the "Giants Graves" as they were replaced by a zig-zag path when the trees in the area were felled, but the mountains and glens, the burns and the beaches will never change, and there will always be happy crowds tumbling off the ferries to enjoy their holidays on Arran.

Puffins

White Deer Calf.

Black Grouse

Otters ~ once rarely seen ~ are now much more numerous

Black Guillemot

On your way round the island, you will see road signs warning drivers to look out for squirrels ~ The red squirrels do not have to compete with the grey ones (which never reached the island) but too many were getting run over by cars.

A most unusual event has been the sighting of a white deer calf on the Arran moors, where the black grouse is also breeding, after an abscence of 30 years.

Since the rats were removed from Ailsa Craig the numbers of puffins on the Firth of Clyde have increased. They do not nest on Arran, but can sometimes be seen from the shore or the ferry

If you were on Arran in 2011, you may have seen some of the competitors in the "Tall Ships Race"

We have added a few extra pages to describe other recent events which we hope you will find interesting. One thing is certain. You will want to come back again because the island is somewhere very special.

HOW TO USE THIS BOOK

We have started in Brodick and worked our way (anti-clockwise) round the island before exploring the two roads crossing Arran ~ the "Ross" and the "String".

You will then have covered all the roads on the island seen all our favourite highlights and learnt a lot about Arran but on this wonderful island there is so much to see that it's impossible to put everything in so we have shown you :—

Grey Heron.

Rock Pipit.

Red Breasted Merganser

Black Throated Diver

Red Throated Diver.

Hen Harrier.

An Arran Mountain
An Arran Glen
A Walk to a Lochan
A Favourite Beach
How to find 20 wild flowers
How to find 20 birds.
A Visit to the Sea Shore
How to learn some Geology
How to learn some Gaelic.
Some of Arran's stories and legends ~ and ~
A few Historical Facts.

We want you to enjoy your holiday here, using this book to help you explore a Scottish island. We want you to find things out, but also have some fun. You might be doing some of the activities on the back cover!

If it is wet, you could start your own note-book, with photo's, postcards, and drawings. You could write your own account of what you have seen and done. In this way the book will become a personal record of YOUR holiday, and you can look back at it later.

Arctic Tern.

Kittiwake

Arran is special, and once you have been, you will want to come again and again, and one day bring your own children. They, in turn, will bring their children, just as we have done. David Hilton

Whiting Bay, 2000.

THE ISLE OF ARRAN

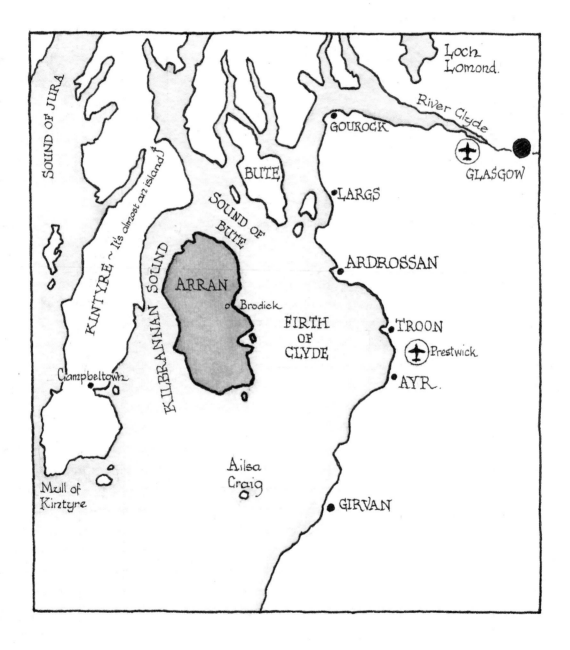

WHERE IS IT ?

ARRAN

OUR FAMILY FAVOURITES

See page 49 for Laurie's favourite in Lochranza.

When I go to Arrn - I like to Meet Grannie Joyce and Grandad Dave at the pier when the Ferry comes in and like Finding out new things about Arran.

orla. age 7

My Visits to Arran

by Ben Atterbury
age 12

I first came to Arran when I was six, I came by plane by myself, and Granny Joyce met me off the plane at Glasgow Airport, we then took a taxi and a train and finally the ferry before we reached Arran, when we got there I loved it. I came back the next year, and the next, and the next, in fact I've been coming back for 7 years and I still haven't seen everything!

I like pony trekking in sannox.

The pony I like best is charley.

I always ride Torquill. I can

rembet some of the others names.

Arran, Lewis, Flin, Torquill, Julius & Callum

Alanna AGE 8

On the Isle of Arran, what i like best is the rock pools in Glen Rosa. they are brilliant. We went there on a lovely hot summer day. My cousins were jumping In off a high rock. It is a lovely Glen to walk up. I hope to go back next year.

Lucy age 10.

On The ILSe OF Arran
MY fAvroute DAY
On Arran WAS When,
We went on QUAd bikesbecAUSe
they and Me went realy fAST

PAUL AGe
171

I LUV ARAAN

Lewie Hilxon age 5

THE SEAS AROUND ARRAN

Herring Gull

However you start your journey, you will reach Arran by ferry. This is the "Caledonian Isles". She (ships are always female) sails from Ardrossan to Brodick. She can carry 1,000 passengers and 120 cars.

Even before you get to Brodick you will see some of the island's wildlife. There will be gulls following the ship. You might also see Dolphins, Porpoises, and even a Basking Shark~ Even though these are the largest of the shark family, they are quite harmless!

Dolphin

Porpoises are smaller than Dolphins!

Basking Shark

THE SEAS AROUND
ARRAN

The first car ferries ran in 1954.
Before that it was rather
difficult to bring a car across
for your holiday. Many people
hired bikes when they arrived
on Arran.
You can still do this!

Before the car
ferries there were
paddle steamers.
There is only one
left now ~ "The
Waverley" You might be
able to have a pleasure
cruise on her.

~ And before steamships
were invented, people
had to cross in sailing
boats. This could take
two or three days if
the wind was in the
wrong direction!

BRODICK

Brodick, nestling in a superb setting beneath the mountains, is the first place on the island you will see. This is where the ferry comes in, and where buses leave for all parts of the island.

There are many shops and hotels in Brodick. You can hire bikes and boats or play crazy golf and putting. Across the bay, with its fine sandy beach, you can see Brodick Castle which is floodlit at night.

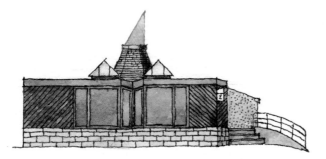

TOURIST INFORMATION

Quite early in your holiday it's a good idea to visit the Tourist Information Centre - It's just opposite the Ferry Terminal.
Here you can find out about activities and places to visit. Many of these are in this book, but we haven't given the admission fees or opening hours because these change from time to time and it's better to get up-to-date information from the Tourist Office

Tourist Information also helps people to find somewhere to stay - Hotels, guest houses, and holiday cottages.

The people are very helpful and friendly. and will help with your holiday plans.

THE ARRAN BANNER

EVERY SATURDAY

The Island's Newspaper Tells you 'What's On'

The local paper not only tells you all the news ~ so that you can feel part of the island while you are here ~ but there is a whole page of events ~ something for every day of the week!

The Story of the Banner

The first issue of the "Arran Banner" was published on the 4th of March, 1974. 98% of the people on Arran read the "Banner" This has earned it a place in the GUINNESS BOOK OF RECORDS. No other local paper is so well read in its own area!

ARRAN for GOLFERS

Brodick golf course is at the end of the village ~ on the right.
You could have a golfing holiday on Arran and
play a different course every day of the week!
Arran has seven courses, and they all welcome
visitors. If that seems rather a lot for a small island,
golf is very popular with islanders and holiday-
-makers alike. Lamlash is the oldest course (1889),
There have been even more courses in the past - at
Pirnmill, Kildonan and Corriecravie.

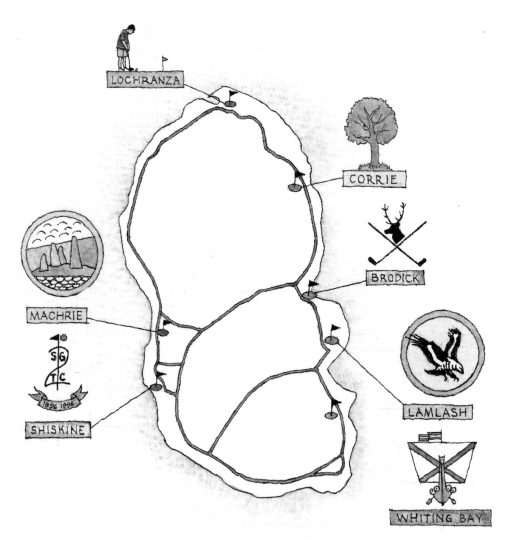

THE ARRAN SCHOOLS

On your way out of Brodick you will see Brodick Primary School on the left hand side of the road.

The statue in front of the school is of William Alexander Anthony Archibald, 11th Duke of Hamilton. He gave the land and the money to build the school.

There are six other primary schools on Arran. Each has a different coloured sweater. One High School in Lamlash serves the whole island.

BRODICK CORRIE PIRNMILL SHISKINE KILMORY WHITING BAY LAMLASH

ARRAN'S
MILESTONES

However you travel round the island, look out for the milestones! Here is the first one. You will find it just after the Museum, but on the opposite side, and before you get to the String Road junction

We think that the milestones would be placed in position when the road round Arran was finally completed about 150 years ago.

If you travel about two miles towards Corrie, you will find the last stone ~ There isn't a stone that says "0 miles".

The people who put up the milestones came round the other way!
There are more milestones on the String Road and the Ross Road which run across the island.

ARRAN HERITAGE MUSEUM

The Museum has been a farm, a smithy, and a school at different times.

Here you can see :—

How old farm machinery was used

How people travelled by land and sea

How Arran lived in war-time

How the rocks were formed

How PRE-HISTORIC people lived

How an Arran cottage looked round about 1920.

BRODICK CASTLE

Brodick has one of the nicest little castles in Scotland. You may already have seen a picture of it on the Royal Bank of Scotland's £20 note!

The OPEN TOP BUS runs between Brodick Pier and the castle in summer.

BRODICK CASTLE

The Castle was built between 1300 and 1844

In the Castle ground you will find :-

PLEASANT WALKS along marked trails

COUNTRYSIDE CENTRE and NATURE ROOM

ADVENTURE PLAYGROUND

BAVARIAN SUMMER HOUSE - Decorated inside with pine cones.

ICE HOUSE - used to preserve food before refrigeration

TEA ROOM and SHOP

BRODICK CASTLE
AND THE NATIONAL TRUST

For many centuries the castle (and most of the island!) belonged to the Dukes of Hamilton and their descendants. About 50 years ago, they gave it to the National Trust for Scotland.

Today the National Trust look after the castle and its surrounding land, so that we can all visit and enjoy it. You might want to become a member of the Trust. (Anyone can join)

Highland cattle help to keep the grasslands in good condition

The Bavarian Summerhouse.

GOATFELL and GLEN ROSA also belong to the National Trust. Their Rangers and voluntary helpers work to maintain the footpaths and protect the wildlife.

MOUNTAINS FOR PEOPLE [An N.T.S. PROJECT]

The hill paths on Goatfell, and in Glen Rosa are so popular that they would become boggy in some places and dangerous in others if they were not looked after very carefully. This is done by the National Trust, but in such a way that the paths still look completely natural.

In 2010, a team of men worked on the upper part of Glen Rosa. It would have taken them up to 6 hours each day just to walk to work, so the Trust provided huts where the men could live. They were flown in by helicopter and had beds, toilets, cookers, fridges and electric light. Everybody who walks in the glen will appreciate this work.

AN ARRAN MOUNTAIN

GOAT FELL is the highest mountain on Arran. It is also the easiest to climb, because there is a good path which starts from the sawmill on the main road, just before you come to the castle entrance. Only the last part of the route (just below the summit), is steep and rocky. But be very careful. All the mountains are dangerous in bad weather. Even if it is fine when you set off, take food and drinks, warm and waterproof clothing and strong shoes or boots. Allow all day to get up and down Goatfell.

HAPPY CLIMBING!

GOATFELL SUMMIT

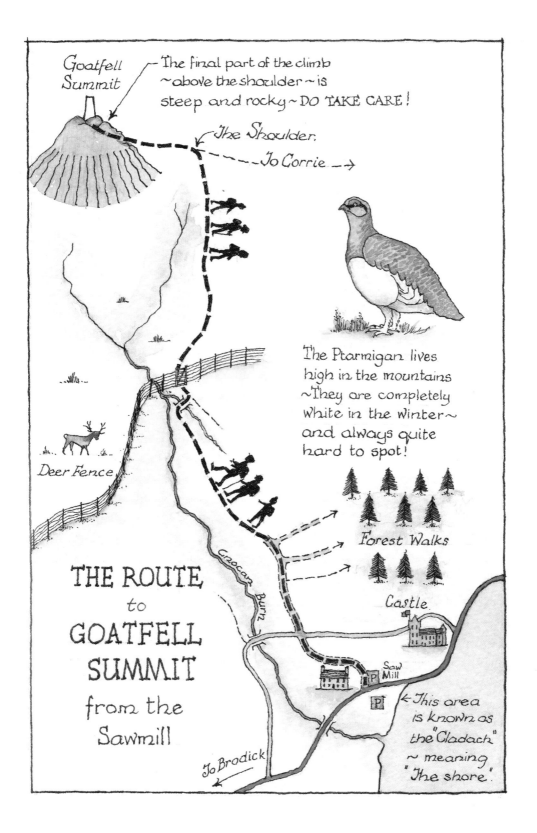

Goatfell Summit

The final part of the climb ~above the shoulder~ is steep and rocky~ DO TAKE CARE!

The Shoulder.

To Corrie →

The Ptarmigan lives high in the mountains ~They are completely white in the winter~ and always quite hard to spot!

Deer Fence

Forest Walks

Castle

Crocan Burn

THE ROUTE to GOATFELL SUMMIT from the Sawmill

Saw Mill

This area is known as the "Cladach" ~ meaning "The shore".

To Brodick

AN ARRAN GLEN

A GLEN is a narrow valley with steep sides. A broad valley is a STRATH
GLEN ROSA is quite near Brodick. A good path goes a long way up the glen. You can see the mountains all

around you on the way up ~ then you have a different view on the way down. It's a good place to see RED DEER and hear them roaring in the autumn.

If the weather is kind, there is a lot of fun to be had in the rock pools. Many people say this is one of the most beautiful glens in Scotland.

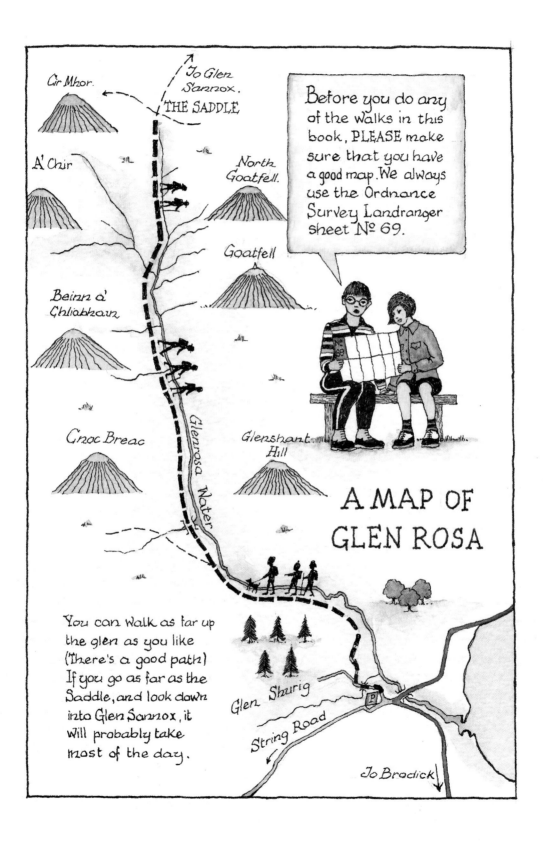

Cir Mhor.

To Glen Sannox.

THE SADDLE

A' Chir

North Goatfell.

Goatfell

Before you do any of the walks in this book, PLEASE make sure that you have a good map. We always use the Ordnance Survey Landranger sheet Nº 69.

Beinn a' Chliabhain

Cnoc Breac

Glenshant Hill

Glenrosa Water

A MAP OF GLEN ROSA

You can walk as far up the glen as you like (There's a good path) If you go as far as the Saddle, and look down into Glen Sannox, it will probably take most of the day.

Glen Shurig

String Road

To Brodick

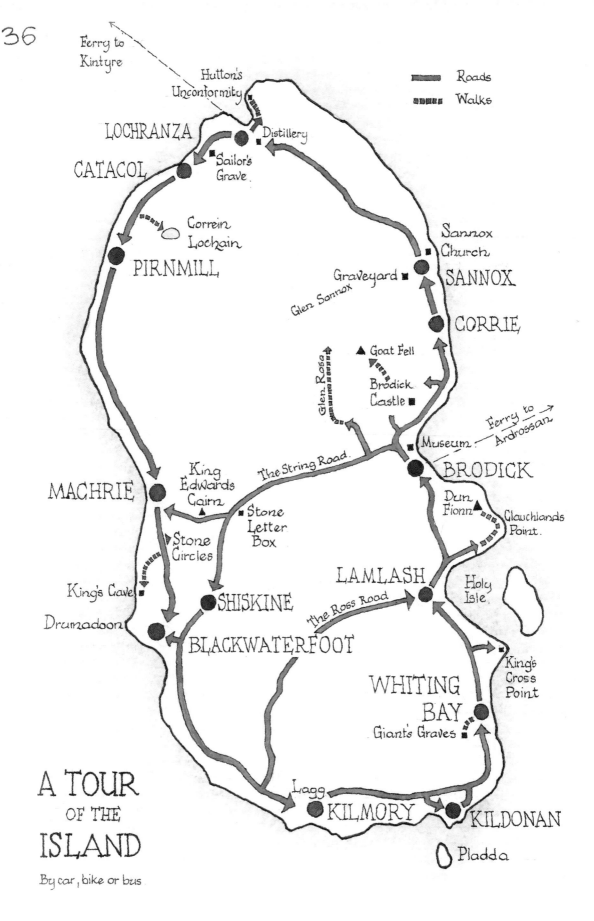

Ferry to Kintyre

Hutton's Unconformity

Roads
Walks

LOCHRANZA
Distillery
CATACOL
Sailor's Grave

Correin Lochain

PIRNMILL

Sannox Church
Graveyard
SANNOX
Glen Sannox

CORRIE

Goat Fell

Brodick Castle

Ferry to Ardrossan

Museum

MACHRIE
King Edwards Cairn
The String Road
BRODICK

Dun Fionn
Clauchlands Point

Stone Letter Box

Stone Circles

King's Cave
LAMLASH
Holy Isle

Drumadoon
SHISKINE
The Ross Road

BLACKWATERFOOT

WHITING BAY
King's Cross Point

Giant's Graves

A TOUR OF THE ISLAND

By car, bike or bus

Lagg
KILMORY
KILDONAN

Pladda

THE JOURNEY BEGINS

Now you have had a look around Brodick, and perhaps sampled Arran's Glens and Mountains, it's time to set off on our journey round the island.

We begin by heading north towards Corrie [The home of this replica Viking longship]

On the way you will pass "Duchess Court" This used to be the "Home Farm" which supplied the castle with produce. Now it is an interesting little shopping centre.

CORRIE

Corrie is a pretty seaside village with its whitewashed cottages and neat gardens at the foot of the mountains. It has always been popular with artists, many of whom once lived above the village at High Corrie.

This area was once famous for its stone quarries. You can still see where some of them were ~ behind the houses where you enter the village, and behind the Village Hall, although they are now very overgrown. Red and white sand--stones were quarried for building on the island and also sent to the mainland, and even the Isle of Man. Limestone was mined underground to make lime for local use.

CORRIE
A TALE OF TWO HARBOURS

The Sandstone Quay

There are two harbours in Corrie. The first one you come to, on the road from Brodick, was built so that sandstone from the local quarries could be loaded on to ships. Next to the toilets you can see the last load of stone that was brought to the harbour in 1928. Nobody came to collect it, and the quarries closed soon afterwards. There are big model sheep to tie your boat to. It is said to be bad luck to tie up to the black one!

The other (older) harbour is where the "Viking Boat" is kept. This is a modern replica. It is used every year in the "Viking Festival," and also when the Battle of Largs is re-enacted.

The Old Harbour

CORRIE

THE DOCTORS BATH

You can find the bath on the shore - opposite a house called "Averton"

The bath was made for Dr. MacCredie. He retired to the house called "CROMLA" around 1830. He had spent many years in India and some of his Indian servants came to Arran with him. He believed that bathing in sea~ ~water was good for his health!

THE FERRY ROCK

The Ferry Rock is near the Corrie Hotel. There was never a pier at Corrie - even when the steamers called at nearly every village. Passengers were ferried ashore by rowing boat.

THE BOULDERS......

BETWEEN CORRIE AND SANNOX......

You will see some big granite boulders on either side of the road. These were brought down from the mountains by glaciers in the Ice Ages.

Geologists call these ERRATICS because they are "out of place". First on the right, leaving Corrie, is the

ELEPHANT ROCK

Next, on the left, we see the CAT STONE. This name has nothing to do with cats! The old Gaelic name was CLACH A' CHATH ~ the stone of the fight! There was a small battle here ~ about 400 years ago

Just as we come into Sannox, the ROCKING STONE is on the right. We HAVE been told you CAN make it rock, but only if you put your hand on it in EXACTLY the right place!

SANNOX

Sannox is a mile or so beyond Corrie at the entrance to Glen Sannox. Just beyond the village a road on the right leads to the North Sannox Picnic Area. This is a delightful place to picnic, with sea views (You <u>might</u> see gannets diving, or dolphins leaping) There are picnic tables and toilets. From here a forestry track leads to the "Fallen Rocks" where a landslide took place, just over 200 years ago.

The Fallen Rocks

SANNOX

THE GOATFELL MURDER

A little way up the cart track that leads into Glen Sannox you will find the graveyard where Edwin Rose is buried. He set off to climb Goatfell one summer evening - over 100 years ago - with another young man he had met on holiday - John Watson Laurie He was never seen alive again, but his body was found three weeks later. Did he fall or was he pushed? - Laurie was tried for murder and spent the rest of his life in prison. Edwin's tombstone is a simple granite boulder from the mountain where he died.

SANNOX CHURCH ~ is up the lane

opposite the entrance to the golf club. It is the second oldest church on the island, built in 1822. In 1829 most of the people here left for Canada. ~ The landowner wanted to "clear" the area for sheep farming The church is usually open. Inside you can see pictures showing the "clearances" The Sannox people built another church ~ just like this - in Canada!

SANNOX and THE MEASURED MILES.

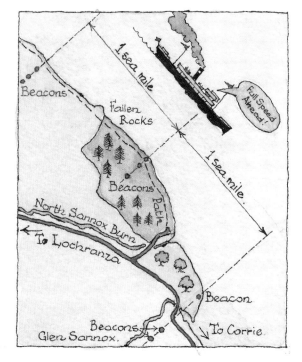

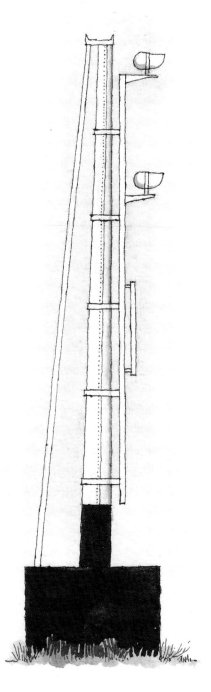

On the way to the Fallen Rocks and also in Glen Sannox, you may notice tall white marker posts with lights [called beacons]. There is another set beyond the Fallen Rocks. If you were to draw a line through each set and extend it out to sea, these lines would be 1 sea mile apart – a little longer than a land mile [see map]. These measured miles were used for testing the speed of ships that had been built or repaired in the Clyde shipyards.

LOCHRANZA

The road from Sannox to Lochranza goes over an area of high ground known as the <u>Boguille</u> (you can guess what that means!). This was the last part of Arran where peat was dug for use as a fuel. You can still see the hollows where this took place. On this road you may see red deer on the hillsides ~ and golden eagles if you are lucky. Lochranza Village is spread on either side of its loch like a horseshoe. Deer and sheep roam freely through the village and on the golf course. You will see that most of the houses have very high garden fences to keep the deer out ~ otherwise they would soon eat all the flowers and vegetables!

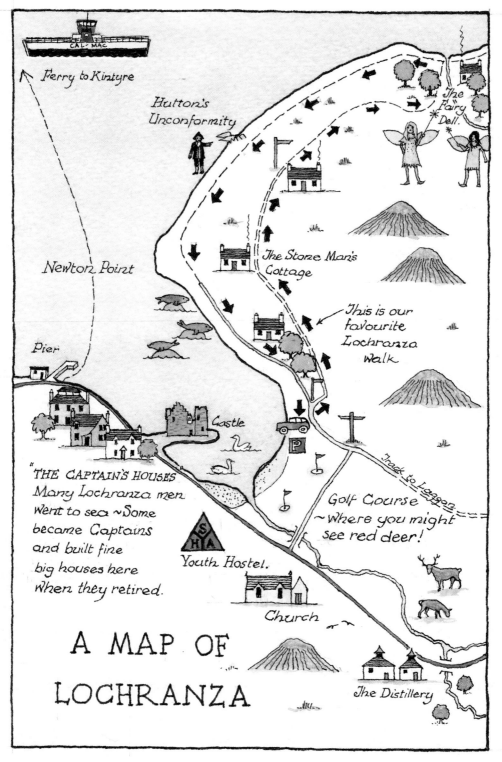

Ferry to Kintyre

Hutton's Unconformity

The Fairy Dell.

Newton Point

The Stone Man's Cottage

This is our favourite Lochranza Walk

Pier

Castle

Track to Laggan

"THE CAPTAIN'S HOUSES
Many Lochranza men
went to sea ~Some
became Captains
and built fine
big houses here
when they retired.

Youth Hostel.

Golf Course
~where you might
see red deer!

Church

A MAP OF
LOCHRANZA

The Distillery

EAGLES and BUZZARDS.

~And how to tell the difference !

It's always exciting to see a Golden Eagle, and LOCHRANZA is one of the most likely places to spot them. They fly very high, and often in pairs. When the distillery was being built, a pair of eagles nested nearby. Eagles don't like to be disturbed~they may abandon their eggs ~ so building work was stopped until the chicks were old enough to leave the nest.

BUZZARDS are much more common than eagles, and are often mistaken for them However, they are much smaller and often lighter in colour with more rounded wings. They call to each other more than eagles, who are usually silent. They often perch on roadside fences ~ something that eagles never do.

THE ISLE OF ARRAN DISTILLERY

You can't miss the Distillery in Lochranza!
Although this is the newest distillery in Scotland
[1995] it has the traditional copper-covered
"pagodas" on the roof. It's also the second
smallest of Scotland's distilleries.

It takes a long time to make whisky ~ It can't even
be called "Whisky" till it's 3 years old ~ and the good
ones are much older ~ but the ingredients are
very simple ~ Barley, Yeast, and water from the
mountain streams. If you want to learn more,
and see the whisky being made, there are guided
tours of the distillery. Ask at the Visitor Centre.

LOCHRANZA

Before 1843 there were no roads into Lochranza. It was easier to come and go by sea!
Most Lochranza men were sailors + fishermen.

This window in the church shows us what was really important in peoples lives. Navigation was taught in the primary school.

The school is now the Outdoor Centre, where you can borrow a key to visit the church and see the window

The church is the oldest one on the island that is still in use. [There are ruins of a much older one in Lamlash]

LOCHRANZA CASTLE

There has been a castle here since the 9th century, when the Vikings built one, but the castle you see today was mostly built in the 14th and 15th centuries to keep the Vikings out!

The castle was badly damaged in a big storm in 1897 and has been a ruin ever since.

The castle is usually open during the day.

Also at Lochranza you can see the smaller Arran ferry, which sails to Claonaig (call it "Kloo-nik") on the Mull of Kintyre. She carries 149 passengers and 18 cars

I have been coming to Arran every year since I was three months old, and every year one of my highlights has been going up to the stoneman's workshop at Lochranza, and my Granny has bought me a stone creature every time (I now have so many my room is covered with them) I have many turtles, a snowman, a santa, two snails, a cat and a mouse. Sometimes it is really windy at the stoneman's cottage and if you look down at the sea it looks like little ripples and sometimes when the ferry goes along it looks like a little toy boat. We have made sort of friends with the "Stoneman" and it is fun to see him work

I am going to be coming still for as long as I can and when I am old this will be one of my fondest memories of Arran.

By Laurie Atterbury 11

A LITTLE GEOLOGY

Just over 200 years ago Dr. James Hutton, an Edinburgh scientist, was looking at the rocks just north of Lochranza.

He noticed that there were two different types of rock, lying at completely different angles, and worked out that these must have been made at very different times ~ millions of years different! So the earth must have been much older than anybody had thought. This rock formation is called "HUTTONS UNCONFORMITY

Red sandstone ~ about 300,000,000 years old sloping towards the sea

Very old schists~ about 600,000,000 years ~ all sloping inland.

HUTTON'S UNCONFORMITY
HOW AN UNCONFORMITY IS MADE

① Rocks laid down as layers of sediment.

② Rocks are heated and folded as the continents move

③ The tops of the folds are worn away by ice and weather.

④ Fresh rocks are laid down on top ~ and worn away again

You can walk to the unconformity from the last house on the Newton Shore ~ where the road ends. This will take 15~20 minutes. The path is rough and boggy in places. Somebody has helpfully made a little stone circle by the path to help you find the unconformity. Turn left here, and walk straight down to the rocks on the shore.

← To the Unconformity.

THE SAILOR'S GRAVE

THE SAILORS GRAVE
HERE LIES
JOHN McLEAN
DIED
12 AUGUST
1854

Between Lochranza and Catacol, a rough track cuts across open ground on the left hand side of the road

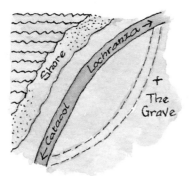

Here you will find the "Sailor's Grave". John McLean was a seaman who died on the way home from the Far East. His last wish was <u>NOT</u> to be buried at sea.

The ships Captain asked for permission to bury him at Lochranza, but this was refused as John had died of cholera — a very infectious disease. His friends had to row him ashore and bury him secretly in this lonely place

CATACOL

THE TWELVE APOSTLES

These twelve cottages at Catacol are all alike ~ except for the upstairs windows! There is a story that these were fishermen's cottages, and if a family wanted to call someone back from the sea ~perhaps for a birth or death in the family ~ they would put a lamp in the upstairs window. The shape would tell the fishermen who it was that needed to go back home.

Whether this story is true or not we know that the cottages were built in 1863 for people who had to leave Glen Catacol to make room for deer-hunting. They preferred to leave the area rather than move into the new houses, which stood empty for two years until they were let to people who were "strangers to the district". They may have been fishermen ~ so perhaps the first story is true!

Did you notice that there are only 12 houses ~ but 13 chimneys? The one at the right-hand end is a dummy ~ to make the whole terrace look better.

A WALK TO A LOCHAN

A LOCHAN is a small LOCH. There is a good path to Correin Lochain which starts from the road between Catacol and Pirnmill.
You will see good views across KILBRANNAN SOUND to KINTYRE as you come down

CORREIN LOCHAIN
A MAP FOR THE WALK

↑ *To Lochranza*

Stepping Stones

Deer Fence

Thunderguy

↙ *To Pirnmill*

The path is steep and rocky in places after you have crossed the burn for the second time. The lochan is Coire Fhionn Lochan (Little Loch of the Fair Corrie). Correin Lochain is the hollow in which it lies

Coire Fhionn Lochan

Meall Biorach (Pointed Hill)

Correin Lochain

HEATHER HONEY

On a warm summer's day you will smell the heather and hear the bees as they collect nectar to make ......

...... HEATHER HONEY!

MORE WILD FLOWERS for you to find on Arran.

Early Purple Orchid.

Meadow Sweet

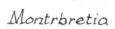

Montrbretia

Foxglove.

Gorse,
or Whin.

Honeysuckle.

PIRNMILL,

HOW THE VILLAGE GOT ITS NAME ~ In the 1800's the hillsides around Pirnmill were planted with birch and beech trees. Which are good woods for making PIRNS (or bobbins) used for cotton spinning in the mills of Paisley. This is what a pirn looks like ⟶ FULL SIZE!

This house used to be the mill where pirns were made.

THE PIRNMILL SUFFRAGETTE

Women finally won the right to vote in 1918

A STORY OF FLORA DRUMMOND

Although she was born in Manchester, Flora grew up in Pirnmill, where her mother had come from, and studied in Glasgow.

At that time ~ about 100 years ago ~ the laws of the country were very unfair to women. Only men could vote ~ and men got all the important jobs!

As a young woman, Flora joined the Suffragettes. a group of women who were trying to change this.

She was such a good organiser she was called "The Little General". She was sent to prison more

than once during her campaign.

At a demonstration in Glasgow, a police--man accused her of "coming from the south to cause trouble". He must have been very suprised when she replied in the Gaelic of her childhood home.

*"That's wrong, I'm an Arran lady"

PIRNMILL THE LITTLE TIN CHURCH

This little church stands in a field, just north of the village. Buildings like this are still quite often seen in country districts. They are known as "Mail Order" buildings. They could be ordered from a catalogue and delivered to the site in sections ~ timber inside and corrugated iron (sometimes called "wiggly tin!") on the outside. This was a quick and economical way to build a church or village hall or some other community building.

CHURCH OF SCOTLAND

Church of Scotland
Lochranza & Pirnmill
Parish of North Arran

Minister: Rev Angus Adamson BD
Tel 302334
Parish Assistant Mrs Jean Hunter BD
Tel 860580.
Session Clerk Mr Peter Emsley
Tel 860232

Sunday Service 10.45 a.m

In 2008 a new bell was given to the church. It came from an older church on the mainland and is itself much older than this little church

MACHRIE MOOR
THE STANDING STONES

We shall never know why the Stone Circles were placed on Machrie Moor about 4,000 years ago. Were they observatories, so that people could tell the seasons from where the sun rose and set each day? Or were they for religious ceremonies, or burial places?
YOU CAN FIND OUT MORE FROM THE INFORMATION
BOARDS ON THE MOOR

The first circle of the main group is a double one. Can you find the stone with a hole through the corner? Fingal the Giant used to tie his giant dog to this when he grew tired of excersising him!

THE STONE CIRCLES OF ARRAN

There are ten stone circles on the island as well as many single standing stones.

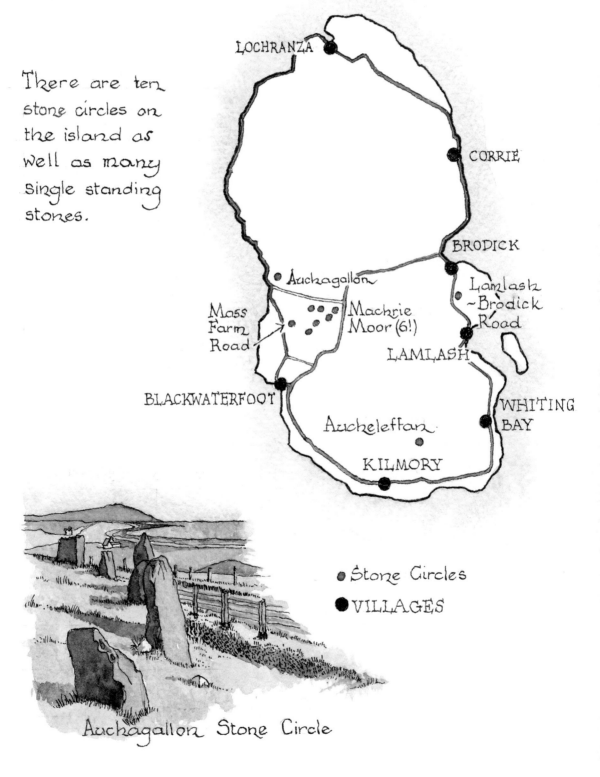

LOCHRANZA

CORRIE

BRODICK

Lamlash ~Brodick Road

Auchagallon

Moss Farm Road

Machrie Moor (6!)

LAMLASH

BLACKWATERFOOT

WHITING BAY

Aucheleffan

KILMORY

• Stone Circles

● VILLAGES

Auchagallon Stone Circle

THE KING'S CAVE
HOW TO GET THERE

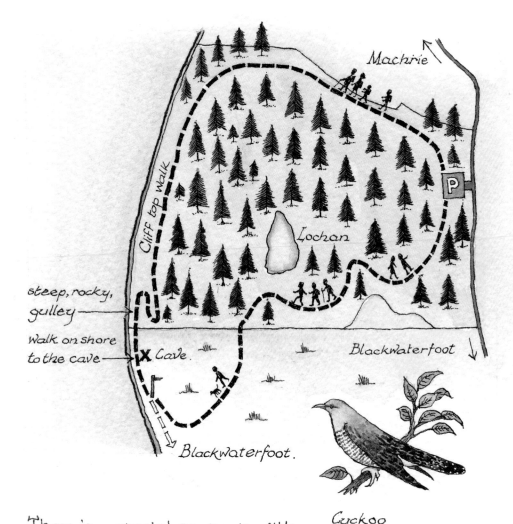

There is a special car park, with
information board, on the main road for people visiting
the cave. A new circular path has made this into a
truly glorious walk. We found 20 wild flowers (at
the end of May) and heard the cuckoo the moment
we started. With a picnic on the beach, and some time
in the cave, this will make a good half day walk.

THE KING'S CAVE

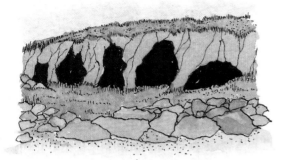

Between the "steep rocky gulley" and the cave, the walk is along the shore.

This is what geologists call a "raised beach" ~ land which was once under the sea. There are many caves which were hollowed out by the force of the waves.

Flag Iris.

KINGS CAVE

Did you bring a torch?

STORIES FROM THE KING'S CAVE

The king was Robert, the Bruce ~ He hid in the cave after losing many battles, and watched a spider spinning its web, which kept breaking ~ but the spider wouldn't give up! Eventually it completed the web and this encouraged Bruce to go on fighting and drive his enemies out of Scotland.

Animal carvings in the right~hand side of the cave A torch will help you to find them ~ and there are more!

AT THE BACK OF THE CAVE

We don't know if the story about the spider is really true, but we do know that people have lived in the cave from very early times ~ some of the carvings are about 1,500 years old. The cave has also been used as a church (see the cross) and a school.

THE KINGS CAVE
AND THE BABY GIANT

Many years before King Robert, a giant called Fingal lived in the cave with his wife. Soon they had a baby giant. When he stretched out he left a footprint on the wall of the cave. The footprint is 90 cm (3 feet) long, so the baby must have been about 540 cm (18 feet) tall. If you keep to the left as you go into the cave you will see the footprint on the opposite wall ~ not too far in, and about 60 cm (2 feet) above a small carved design that looks like this →

BLACKWATERFOOT

Blackwaterfoot has a fine sandy beach, with views across Kilbrannan Sound to Kintyre. There is also a golf course which is very unusual in having twelve holes ~ not the usual nine or eighteen!

SHISKINE

Shiskine is the only village on Arran which is not on the coast. It lies in the Shiskine Valley, near Blackwaterfoot, and surrounded by some of the best farming land on the island.

BLACKWATERFOOT

When you see the little harbour at Blackwaterfoot,
It's hard to believe it was once used by steamships, ---
but the wee Clyde "puffers" used to call regularly till the
1920's. They would bring in cargoes like coal or drain-
pipes, and take away cattle or potatoes. When more
lorries came onto the roads it was easier to bring
everything into Brodick, and over the "String" road.
The author, Neil Munro, wrote a whole set of stories
about a puffer and its crew. These are called the
"Para Handy Tales", and some of them have been
on T.V.

THE CLIFFS OF
DRUMADOON

["Ridge of the Fort" in Gaelic].

These cliffs were the end of a lava flow in volcanic times. You can reach them by walking along the shore from Blackwaterfoot and across a corner of the golf course ~ but be careful not to get in the way of the golfers,

Fulmar

You may see FULMARS nesting on the cliffs. They have very noticeable nostrils on top of their beaks. They <u>always</u> squat, and <u>never</u> stand up.

GANNETS

can also be seen flying off ~ shore. They plunge into the sea from a great height to catch their fish.

Gannet

BLACKWATERFOOT to KILMORY

On this part of the journey you will pass through Lagg (Gaelic for "The Hollow") This sheltered spot has palm trees and the Lagg Inn. This is the oldest inn on the island (over 200 years old)

There is a pleasant walk from here by the Kilmory Water to the Torrylinn Chambered Cairn ~ the remains of a pre-historic tomb. The Arran Creamery, where cheese is made, is a little farther along the road, towards Kildonan.

The Lagg Inn.

THE LOST KINGDOM
UNDER THE SEA

Arran's only cliff-top road is a mile or two south of Blackwaterfoot on your way round the island.

Old legends tell of a lost kingdom under the sea. If you look down, you will see the churches and palaces and the people going about their daily business. However, all this becomes invisible if there's even the slightest ripple on the surface! One story tells of a strange man with a coach and four horses who boarded a ship in Ayr Harbour, saying he wanted to go to Campbeltown. They disappeared over the side when they were above his home in the lost kingdom.

KILDONAN
SEALS and DYKES.

On the shore at
Kildonan you will see some
interesting things ~ If the tide is not
too high, (or too low!), there will be lots of seals. One
of our grandchildren counted over 120!
Other interesting features are the dykes ~ These
are ribs of rock running out to sea. They are
harder than the rocks on either side, which have
been worn away. Near to the Village Hall there
is a natural harbour formed by two of these
dykes.

KILDONAN

AND THE
CLARK
FAMILY

"DRIMLA LODGE"

On the Shore road at Kildonan you will see a house built of red bricks, with a red tiled roof.
It's quite different from the other Arran houses! This was built in 1901 for the Clark family, who were more famous for making Clark's shoes!

The Clarks also presented a bell to Kildonan Church When this closed, the bell was placed in the wall, just outside the Village Hall.

KILDONAN CASTLE

This castle was built about 1400 for "Black John Stewart ~ a son of King Robert III. Today it's just a ruin, and <u>very</u> dangerous Don't go too near!

AND A BIG SANDY BEACH!

Towards the east end of the village, where the road curves inland, you will find steps leading down to our own favourite Arran beach

THE SEASHORE

Shore Crab.

No holiday on Arran would be complete without a day on the seashore. You will find all sorts of interesting creatures in the rock pools. Don't try to take them home. They will almost certainly die.

Mussel Shells.

Pod Razor Shell.

Common Cockle

Limpets   Barnacles.

THE SEASHORE

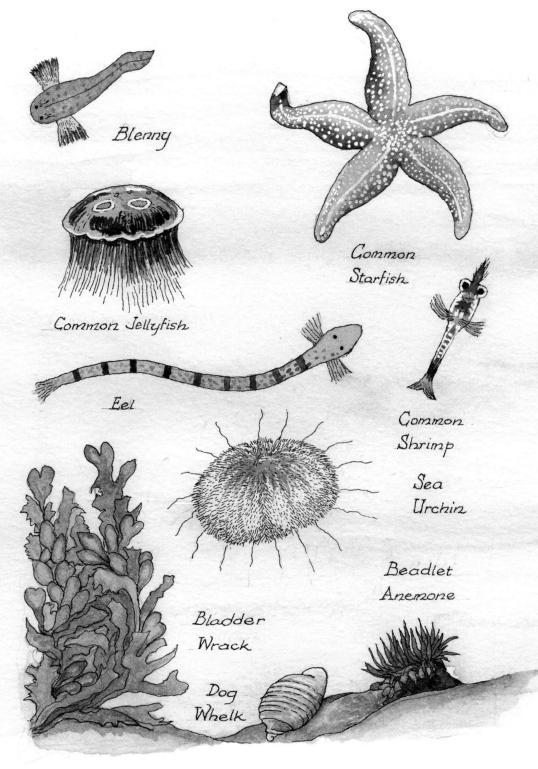

Blenny

Common Jellyfish

Common Starfish

Eel

Common Shrimp

Sea Urchin

Beadlet Anemone

Bladder Wrack

Dog Whelk

KILDONAN
and AILSA CRAIG

From the hill that leads back to the main road - and Whiting Bay ~ you get a good view of the castle, the old Coastguard's lookout, the island of Pladda with its lighthouse, and Ailsa Craig, sometimes called "Paddy's Milestone" ~ it's half way between Ireland and Glasgow.

Curling Stone.

Only thousands of sea birds now live on Ailsa Craig. At one time there was a castle, and there's still a lighthouse. The stone quarries on Ailsa Craig produced the finest curling stones in Scotland. This game ~ it's played on ice ~ has become much better known since Rhona Martin and her team (all from Scotland) won a gold medal for Britain at the Winter Olympics in 2002.

WHITING BAY

Whiting Bay village is spread out along the coast . It is a good. centre for walks to Glenashdale Falls , the Giant's Graves , and King's Cross Point .

When steamers used to call at Whiting Bay it had the longest pier on the Clyde. The D.I.Y shop used to be the pier offices, and the way on to the pier was where the petrol pumps now stand .

The playing fields at Sandbraes are sometimes used as a landing area by rescue helicopters .

WHITING BAY
THE GIANTS GRAVES

The path to the Giant's Graves starts in Whiting Bay, near the bridge over the Glenashdale Burn.

Follow the signposts to the Giants Graves This is how the climb up through the forest used to look _ _ _ _ _
_ _ but see next page!

The graves were made about 5,000 years ago. Many people were buried together in each one. Later on, people had forgotten this, and thought that such large graves must have been for giants!

THE GIANTS GRAVES TODAY

When this book was first written, the way to the Giants Graves was up 315 steps through the woods. The graves were in a clearing in the forest, as you can see on Page 80 (It was all quite spooky in a nice sort of way!) Now the trees have been cut down, and the way to the graves is by a zig ~ ~zag path.

We need not feel too sorry about the trees ~ they were only planted so that they could be cut down later. Most of the timber grown on Arran is used for paper making. Perhaps even this page was once part of an Arran tree! The graves now look much more like they would have done 5,000 years ago. There are new information boards to tell you more about them.

WHITING BAY

GLENASHDALE FALLS

If you return to the main path after visiting the Giants Graves you can continue to Glenashdale Falls.

There's a bridge to cross the burn just above the falls, and you can come back to the village down the other side. There's an old fort on the way. It's about a 5km (3 miles) walk.

Red Campion.

Stitchwort.

Wild Garlic

Bluebells

In spring and early summer you can see Red, White, and Blue flowers on the way up to the falls!

SOMETHING DIFFERENT

In the evenings, our little
grandchildren liked to
watch the lighthouses,
starting with Holy Isle,
then Turnberry (on the mainland), Pladda, and
sometimes as far round as Davaar (on Kintyre).

Each has a different pattern of flashes and intervals
so that sailors can recognise them.

Holy Island	Green Light	Every 3 seconds
Turnberry	White Light	Every 15 seconds
Pladda	White Light x 3	Every 30 seconds
Davaar	White Light x 2	Every 10 seconds

Many parts of the island have no street lighting
so that here, on a clear night, you can see all
the stars in heaven shining on the Isle of Arran.

THE PRINCESS
AND THE
LIGHTHOUSES

Princess Anne has been interested in the Scottish lighthouses since she was five years old, when she visited Tiumpan Head, on the Isle of Lewis, with her mother, the Queen.

In 1993 Anne became Patron of the Northern Lighthouse Board. She takes her duties very seriously, and often joins one of the Board's ships which visit the lighthouses to carry out repairs and maintainance. She hopes to see as many of the lighthouses as possible.

The Princess came to Arran in 2008 to see the lighthouse on Pladda and the two on Holy Isle.

MORE LIGHTHOUSE STORIES

Most of the Scottish lighthouses were built by one family ~

~ the Stevensons, engineers to the Northern Lighthouse Board for four generations.

All the lighthouses are now automatic, but we should remember the lighthouse keepers who kept their lights burning in wild and lonely places. On Holy Island you can see the former keepers cottages and the walled garden where they could grow some fresh vegetables between their turns "on watch".

The Northern Lighthouse Board look after 207 lighthouses in Scotland and the Isle of Man. They use some very sophisticated equipment, such as helicopters and specialised ships ~ "Pharos" and "Pole Star" (which you might sometimes see near Arran). Now there is to be a solar powered light on Pladda!

KINGS CROSS POINT
AND HOW TO GET THERE

The roads to King's Cross are not suitable for parking. If you come by car, it's best to leave it opposite Whiting Bay Church and continue on foot, following the route shown on this map ▰ ▰ ▰ ▰ ▰ ➤

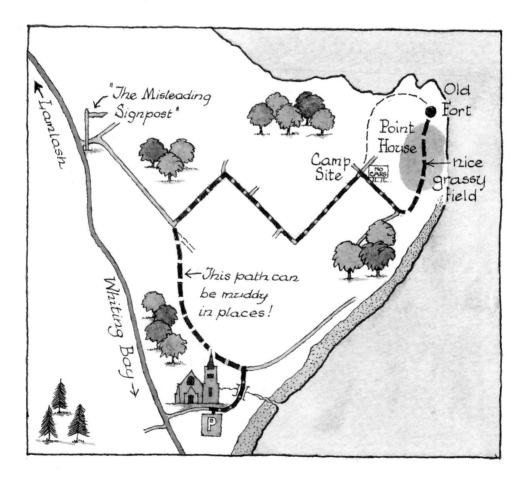

KING'S CROSS POINT

King's Cross Point seems a quiet place today, but it's had its share of exciting events in the past! Now turn to the next page..........

To Turnberry!

KING'S CROSS POINT

Where KING Robert [the Bruce] CROSSED to the mainland in 1307.

There is a signpost on the main road ~ between Whiting Bay and Lamlash. It says "Viking Fort - 1 mile". This isn't quite right. There was a much older fort here - about 2,500 years old from the Iron Age. You can still see part of the walls - but this is what it would have looked like when it was first built ....

The Iron Age fort may already have been 1,000 years old when one of the old Viking chiefs died in this area. His men burnt his body in his own ship. [This was their custom]. You can still see the boat ~ shaped hollow just before you get to the fort.

LAMLASH

Lamlash was a very important naval base in World War II (1939~1945), when submarine crews were trained here. Today, many of the island's affairs are run from Lamlash. Here you will find the Arran High School ~ for pupils from all over the island. The island's hospital is also here, although very ill people may have to be taken to the mainland by helicopter.

Here you will also find ....

The Police Station.

The Fire Station.

The Coastguard Depot.

The Lifeboat Station, and

The Council Offices.

Lamlash Church has a carillon~ a set of bells, which plays tunes before the Sunday Morning Service.

LAMLASH AND THE CLEARANCES

When people left their homes at the time of the Clearances, there were three things they could do :—~~~

Some moved to the the villages on the coast, like Brodick and Lamlash, which grew up at this time, and learnt new trades.

Others went to the Scottish mainland to work in the Clyde shipyards or the Lanarkshire coal mines.

And many sailed away to Canada (the Duke paid half their fares). The monument on the green at LAMLASH tells the story of 86 people from Sannox (see p 35) who sailed to Canada from Lamlash Bay in 1829.

In 1977, some of their descendants returned to make this monument.

The houses in the background were built for estate workers by the 12th Duke of Hamilton in 1894.

The "Clearances" Monument at Lamlash

> Here's an offer you can't refuse!

CANADA (SINGLE)

THE CLEARANCES

The island looked very different 200 years ago. There were no roads or villages. Instead, people lived in little groups of six or eight houses called "clachans" (Gaelic for "the stones") scattered all over the island. They grew their own food and kept a few cows on the surrounding land. Round about 1800 the Duke of Hamilton, who owned most of the island, decided that a few large farms, with lots of sheep, and, later on, some deer to hunt, would be much better. As a result, many people had to leave the island. You can see the ruins of abandoned clachans in many parts of Arran.

THE PREACHERS MOUND

After you have seen the "Clearances" monument, cross the road and look at the small hillock known as the "Preachers Mound".

Before the people from Sannox sailed away to Canada, the Minister from Sannox Church (see page 43) preached to them, telling them to trust God, who would look after them in the New World, quoting the Bible (--- casting all your cares upon Him for He careth for you ----)

(Peter, 1, 5:7)

The men made a small mound for the Minister to stand on. They would have spades (and other tools) with them to use in Canada ~ but there is another story ~ that the mound was originally a pile of hats which the men had taken off for the service! Although the village green has been much altered over the years, this mound has always been preserved.

SOME ARRAN FACTS

DID YOU KNOW ......

That there are no grey squirrels, stoats, weasels or moles on Arran?

But there are red squirrels, golden eagles, and 2,000 red deer (and just over 4,000 people)

That Arran used to send sand to Saudi Arabia?
(It was a special sand used in water filters)

That McKelvie Road in Lamlash is named after Donald McKelvie O.B.E who developed many kinds of Arran potatoes ~ including Arran Chieftain, Arran Pilot and Arran Banner?

That when the Government of Cyprus wanted to introduce potatoes to that island, they chose the Arran varieties?

Arran's trusty lifeboat, "The Boy's Brigade" is stationed at Lamlash?

HARRY POTTER AND THE SECRET OF LAMLASH CEMETERY!

Lamlash Cemetery is high on the hill behind the village. In the oldest part of the cemetery, ~ within the stone walls ~ you will find the grave of the Reverend Colin Campbell, who died in 1882 The headstone is white, and in three parts.

Many of Colin's family are buried with him ~ but not his son Dugald, who became a doctor in London

Dugald was to be the GREAT GRANDFATHER of J.K. ROWLING ~ who wrote the HARRY POTTER stories!

When you are in an old cemetery it can be interesting to read what is written on the headstones.

You will see that, although most people had quite large families, many children died when they were still very young.

In Lamlash, many of the men were connected with the sea. You may be able to find the grave of a "pier~master". Many of the monuments contain the names of family members who died at sea or in far~away places.

Also buried at Lamlash is Helen Kelsall Asquith. Her husband, H.H.Asquith was the British Prime Minister from 1908 to 1916. Sadly, Helen died in 1891 whilst on holiday in Lamlash.

You never know who you might find!

HOLY ISLAND

Holy Island is a special island in Lamlash Bay

Long ago it was the home of Saint Molios, whose cave can still be seen there.

Walk past the Lifeboat Station to the jetty to catch the Holy Isle Ferry. The crossing takes about 10 minutes, and _____

_____ This is what you will see when you arrive !

HOLY ISLAND

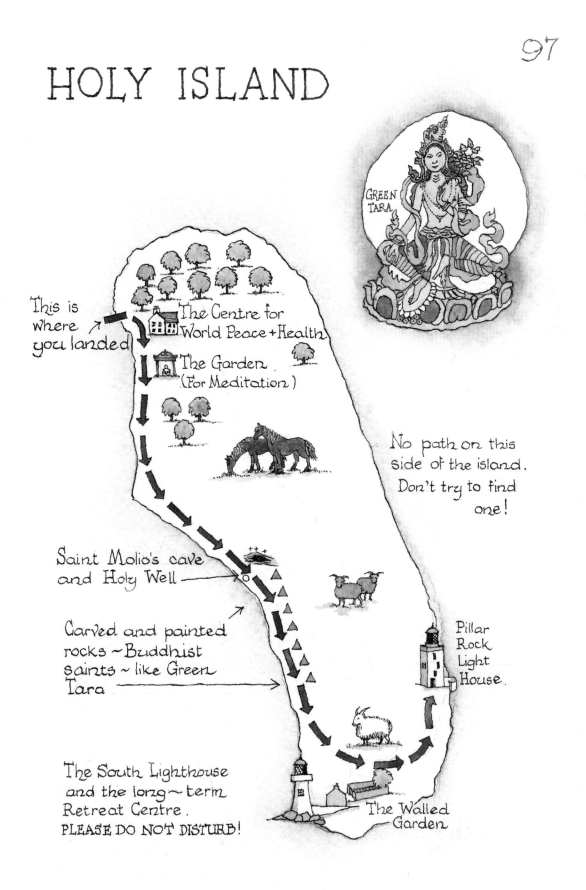

GREEN TARA

This is where you landed

The Centre for World Peace + Health

The Garden (For Meditation)

No path on this side of the island. Don't try to find one!

Saint Molio's cave and Holy Well —

Carved and painted rocks ~ Buddhist saints ~ like Green Tara

Pillar Rock Light House

The South Lighthouse and the long~term Retreat Centre. **PLEASE DO NOT DISTURB!**

The Walled Garden

HOLY ISLAND

Holy Island is now home to a Buddhist community. They believe we should live our lives so as not to harm any living thing.

We suggest an easy walk, following the red arrows on the map as far as the Pillar Rock Lighthouse. Do you notice anything different about this lighthouse? (see p. 98)

On the way, look out for :-
> St Molios' Cave and Well
> The painted rocks
> The walled garden
> Eriskay ponies
> Soay sheep
> Sanaan goats
> Great views of the Clyde + Ailsa Craig

You will have a lovely day here ~ but please be very considerate as many people have come here for peace and quiet.

"May all beings be happy"

MORE ARRAN FACTS

Arran has had many Royal visitors ~Robert the Bruce, Edward VII, the Queen (twice) and Princess Diana

Famous authors who have visited Arran include Sir Walter Scott, Lewis Carroll, and Robert Browning. (but never, ever, Robert Burns!)

Daniel Macmillan, who founded the famous publishing firm of Macmillan, was an Arran farmer who left the island at the time of the clearances. His grandson, Harold, was the Prime Minister of Great Britain from 1957 to 1963.

Jack Mc Connell, who became Scotland's First Minister, grew up at Glenscorrodale Farm, and went to Arran High School.

 BREAKING NEWS!~May 2013~Arran's first blue plaque was fixed to the wall of Lamlash Co-Op. It commemorates the life and work of Donald McKelvie O.B.E ~ the pioneering breeder of Arran potatoes ~ Look out for this!

A WALK TO CLAUCHLANDS POINT

Where the road turns inland towards Clauchlands Farm a track continues towards Clauchlands Point ~ there is a gate and a signpost

On the way to the point it's worth keeping an eye open for interesting birds on the seashore. Curlews and Oystercatchers are often seen here, with Eider Ducks just offshore

Oystercatcher

Curlew

Male

Female

Eider Ducks.

HAMILTON'S ROCK

Although the Hamilton family owned most of Arran for 600 years Hamilton's Rock is the only natural feature named after them.

Common Seal.

Grey Seal

Two kinds of seals can be seen on, or near the rock......
the Common Seal and the (bigger) Grey Atlantic Seal.

Among the many sea-birds you may see Cormorants and Shags. Both spread their wings out to dry after diving to catch fish.

Cormorant

The cormorants and shags look rather alike from a distance, but these pictures may help you to spot the differences.

Shag.

A WALK to DUN FIONN

[The White Fort]

To Brodick

Path

Cairn

Dun Fionn

Forestry Road

P

To Lamlash

The path to Dun Fionn starts on the right hand [east] side of the road from Lamlash to Brodick right at the top of the hill. If you follow the sign posts, first to "Dunfion" and then to the "Forest Walk", you will find yourself walking along the ridge of the Clauchland Hills, with wonderful views to Goatfell,

Holy Island, Lamlash Bay, and the Firth of Clyde. At the highest point on the ridge you will pass a cairn ~ a big pile of stones. You are now about half way to Dun Fionn. On your way through the woods you may see red squirrels and short-eared owls. Unlike most other owls, they hunt by daylight.

An hours walking from the road will bring you to Dun Fionn. You can trace the outline of the old fort by the saucer shaped hollow on top of the hill. There's also a "Trig Point", a concrete pillar used by map makers

On a warm summers day you might enjoy a picnic, listen to the song of the skylark and the humming of the bees and enjoy the smell of the clover. You can now look right down into Brodick Bay and see the white sails of the yachts against a turquoise sea. A tiny ferry sails out at 11·05, 13·50 and 16·40. Sometimes you can hear the bells and announcements on board ship!

Surely this is one of the best views in the world!

THE ROADS ACROSS ARRAN
THE "STRING" AND THE "ROSS"

Our journey round the island has started from Brodick and we have travelled 58 miles in "anti-clockwise" direction.

But there are also two roads ACROSS the island. They are called the STRING ROAD and the ROSS ROAD
The String Road was designed by the famous engineer Thomas Telford and built in 1817. Telford built hundreds of miles of roads all over Britain as well as many bridges and canals.

When the sailors were out at sea, they thought that Arran looked like a badly tied-up parcel, and this road was the string round the middle!

Building the road made it easier for people on the west coast to travel to the market and the ferry in Brodick without having to go right round the island.

Further south, the Ross Road was built in 1821. It runs from Lamlash to Bennecarrigan, and takes its name from a nearby hill.

THE STRING ROAD
SOME THINGS TO SEE

This stone letter box stands at the junction with the Machrie Moor road. The Duke of Hamilton wanted the box to be an ornament to his estate.

The builder brought a stone mason out to build the box, then went on holiday for a week and forgot all about him!

To pass the time the mason covered the box with carvings. These were the "marks" of all the masons working on the island at the time. They would put these on all their tools so that everyone would know who they belonged to.

On the MACHRIE MOOR road, at the edge of a wood, you will find this cairn.

The writing on the big stone tells us King Edward VII had lunch here after a mornings shooting on his visit to Arran in 1902 (There is no truth in the story that ten men held the stag down while he shot it!)

THE ROSS ROAD

The first building you will see from the road will be the big white factory where the Arran jams and mustards are made. You can see these in the factory shop on the other side of the road. The shop was opened by the Princess of Wales in 1989

The Ross road runs down Glen Scorrodale. It is wild, lonely, and beautiful. It is named after the giant Scorri, who once lived here. He used to stop the women on their way to market and steal their eggs and butter.

This went on until all the menfolk got together and chased him out of the glen (There probably <u>was</u> someone called "Scorri", but his name makes us think he was a big Viking, not a giant!).

The Ross road ends at the lonely little church of Bennecarrigan.

BACK IN BRODICK

We have now completed our exploration of
the island, and returned to Brodick,
where our journey began.
If you are here in August, you may be
able to watch the Highland Games at
the Ormidale playing fields.

Another August event
not to be missed is the
Arran Farmer's Show.
This has been held in
the Castle Grounds for
the last two years.

Brodick is a good place to buy souvenirs and
presents before you start your journey home.
There is something for everybody ~ chocolates,
cheese, oatcakes, whiskies and beers, also
aromatics, crafts, and jewellery ~ all made on
the island.

SOME ARRAN PLACE NAMES

Most of the mountain names, except GOATFELL, are in GAELIC. This is a very old language. Only a few people speak it now, but it lives on in many place names.

MOUNTAIN NAMES

The Name	What it means	How to say it
A' Chir	The Comb	Ah Keer
Cir Mhor	The Big Comb	Keer Vore.
Am Binnean	The Little Hill	Am binny-an
Beinn-a'Chliabhain	Hill of the Little Creel.	Ben ah Kleeven
Beinn Bhreac	Speckled Hill	Ben Vreck
Beinn Bharrain	The Baron's Hill	Ben Varen
Beinn Bhiorach	Pointed Hill	Ben Virax
Beinn Nuis	Hill of the Face	Ben Noosh
Beinn Tarsuinn	Cross-wise Hill	Ben Tarsin
Caisteal Abhail.	The Castles.	Kashteel Avall
Ceum na Caillich	The Witches Step.	Kame na Kylie-ak
Cioch na h-Oighe.	The Maiden's Breast	Kee-ok na Hoy
Suidhe Fhearghais	Fergus's Seat	Sooey Fergus.

SOME VILLAGES ALSO HAVE GAELIC NAMES

Corrie	Hollow in the Hills	As spelt
Kildonan	Church of St Donan	"
Kilmory	Church of St Mary	"

A FEW HOUSE NAMES

Many Arran people like to give their house a Gaelic name. Here are just a few you may see.

The Name	What it means	How to say it
Am Fasgadh	The Shelter	Am Faska
Cala-na-Sithe	Haven of Peace	Kalla-na-Shee
Ceol-na-Mara	Music of the Sea	Keeol-na-Mara
Sealladh-na-Mara	Sea View	Shallug-na-Mara
Tigh-na-Mara	House of the Sea	Ty-na-Mara.

SOME NAMES THE VIKINGS LEFT US

Although the Vikings came to fight and rob, many stayed to become good farmers and fine craftsmen Also their place names are quite easy to say. Some names had Gaelic words like "Glen", and "Loch" added later

Goat Fell - Hill of the Goats.
[Glen] Ashdale - Dale of the ash trees.
[Glen] Chalmadale - Hjalmud's Dale
[Glen] Scorrodale - Scorri's Dale
[Glen] Rosa - Glen of the Horses (Hrossa)
[Loch] Ranza - Loch of the Rowan Tree River.
Brodick (was "Bredavik") - Broad Bay.
Sannox (was "Sandvik") - Sandy Bay.
Pladda - Flat Island.

[Gaelic additions in square brackets]

THE BEST THINGS IN LIFE ARE STILL FREE [A PAGE FOR THE GRANNIES]

From an old Hymn

1. I said it in the mea-dow path, I said it on the mountain stairs—
The best things an-y mor-tal hath Are those which ev-ery mor-tal shares.

Lucy Larcom (19th century)

On a beautiful summer's evening Granny Joyce and Paul were walking down Glen Rosa after a happy day at the rock pools. "Can we come again?" said Paul, "But are the rock pools free?" "Oh yes." said Granny Joyce "All day, and every day, and FOR EVER."

*   *   *

MORE OF THOSE BEST THINGS IN LIFE----------

Carpets of Bluebells on the way to Brodick Castle

Tangles of wild flowers in the spring hedgerows

Arran's pure fresh air

Mountains and Glens to explore. A glimpse of deer-watching you!

Our beaches with their rock pools and shells and seals

The ferry~ all lit up for a late evening sailing.

Glorious sunsets over the Mull of Kintyre to stir your soul.

Your grandchild's hot little hand in yours as you discover the

island together, and your heart fills with happiness,

The wee White Rose of Scotland
(Burnet Rose~*Rosa Pimpinellinellifolio*)

112

ARRAN AGAIN !

Sailing for me is always great pleasure,
The wind and the water, the sky and the shore,
All linked together in limitless measure,
To lift up my spirits, feel happy once more.

I went sailing westwards to my special isle,
And wondered how changed I would find my retreat,
For the vision of past can deceive or beguile,
Yet I longed to be back midst wild heather and peat.

My first sight of the hills filled my heart with delight,
Then the woodlands and meadows spread over the land,
Grey seals on the rocks, wheeling seabirds in flight,
Oh this is for me! To be back is just grand.

Betty Stewart.
[Grandma Betty]

FAREWELL.......

Sadly, all holidays on Arran will come to an end. The "Caledonian Isles" has been in the background for so many "Welcoming hugs" and "Good-bye hugs" that take place at Brodick Pier.

Friends and relations wave till they are little dots on the horizon.

A LAST WORD AT THE FERRY

GOOD~BYE, LITTLE COUSINS~UNTIL WE MEET AGAIN

ON ARRAN NEXT YEAR

Also overheard at the ferry..... "But Mummy, we can't go home yet - we haven't finished the book."

We are sure you will have seen many interesting things on your holiday. Perhaps you climbed Goatfell, and when you have your last look at it from the deck of the ferry, you can't quite believe that you ever stood on its top. But, on Arran, there's always more, so------

HASTE YE BACK!

ACKNOWLEDGEMENTS

We would like to thank all the people on the Isle of Arran who have helped and encouraged us in the preparation of this book; especially ----------------

Iain Hendry and Ralston Green, bus drivers, for their unfailing courtesy and for sharing their local knowledge with us.

The Rangers at Brodick Castle Country Park.

H.F Holidays, Altachorvie, Lamlash.

Betty and Mike Koral, "Crafts of Arran", Whiting Bay for reading the first draft and encouraging us to go ahead.

Ruth and Alan Thompson of Lamlash, who conserved Arran's milestones for us all.

Dr. Robin Whitla, who tried to teach David Gaelic

John Roberts, Brodick, for help and advice.

Lucy, for checking that David's writing is readable!

"Last night I dreamed of Arran's shore,
Dreamed of her hills and glens once more,
Dreamed of the sunshine and the rain,
And all my Arran friends again."

Anon.

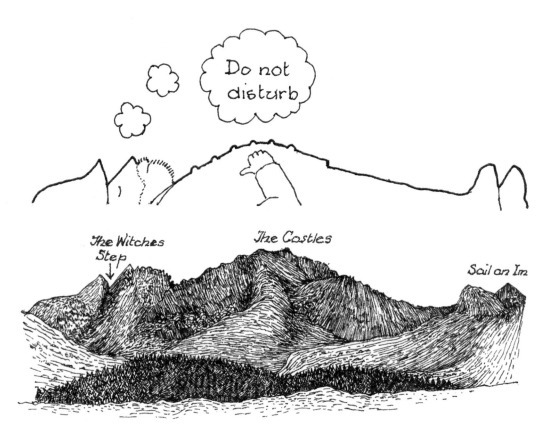

This is the "SLEEPING WARRIOR"
The best place to see him is from the top of
the Boguille ~ looking towards Sannox ~